BITCOIN, NFT AND CRYPTOCURRENCY TRADING FOR BEGINNERS 2021

Blockchain, Cryptocurrency, Wallets, Trading, Leverage, Security & NFTs

Davis Nakamoto

I0492567

Table of contents

1. THE SUDDEN RISE

Bitcoin in 2021 with a market capitalization of over 600 Billion United States Dollar, is already bigger than the revenue of several fortune 500 companies, and even some countries'Gross Domestic Product. A Bitcoin currently trades at over 60,000 United States Dollar, bigger than any share of any company. The sudden rise in the price of Bitcoin is proof that the fiat money we are used to, is outdated, more like how quickly digital camera came in and kicked the ass of the old Polaroid cameras that we were used to in the early 90s.

Take a look at the sudden rise as shown in this graph from Statista 2021.

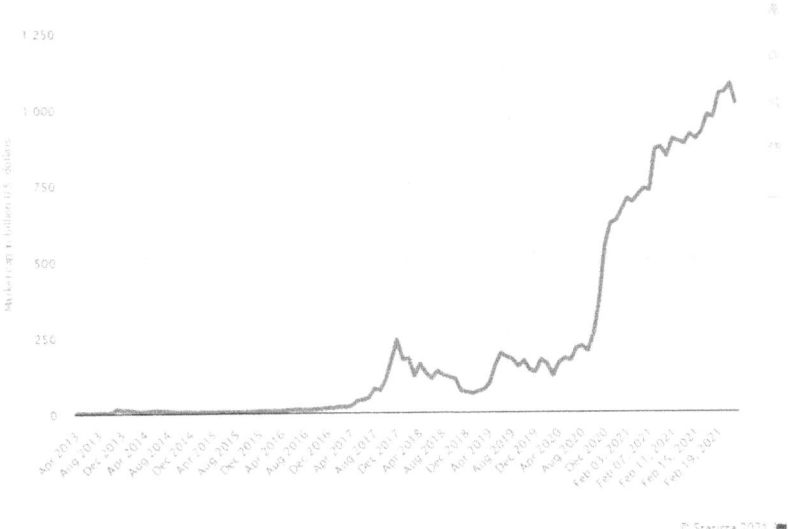

It is believed that, with Bitcoin being limited in supply (only 21 million Bitcoin will ever be in existence), Bitcoin will surpass this price in the long term. If the predictions come to pass, then Bitcoin would be the best store of value – a nice way to save money. Look at that graph and make your own prediction if you are yet to decide.

2. NOTHING LASTS FOREVER

I do not wish to introduce Bitcoin as a money making venture, although there are several opportunities we can take to make money with Bitcoin. Bitcoin, just like every other crypto-currency, enables unregulated cross-border payments. Most governments are just scared of this new trend. They are scared of this free-flow of money because it takes away the power which they had to regulate and manipulate money in the past.

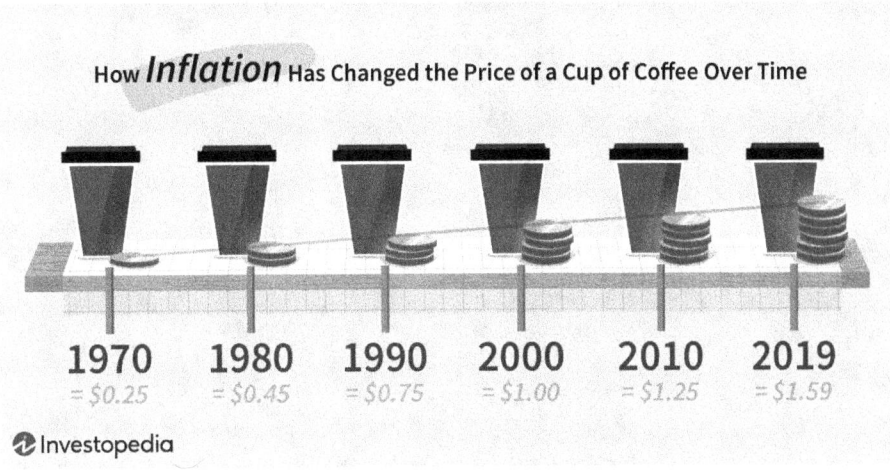

How *Inflation* Has Changed the Price of a Cup of Coffee Over Time

1970	1980	1990	2000	2010	2019
= $0.25	= $0.45	= $0.75	= $1.00	= $1.25	= $1.59

Investopedia

No thanks to the government who continuously pump in new notes into the economy, this manipulation causes money to lose value over time.

A federal reserve or a central bank can go on printing money at a rate faster than economic growth, and this leads to inflation. But what happens in the world of Bitcoin is the opposite – deflation.

This is why people would feel safer to save their money in BTC, the symbol of Bitcoin. The value of Bitcoin has kept on rising, since it was launched. But just like Fiat currencies, Bitcoin will also become outdated soon, especially with the rise of other cryptocurrencies with much better features. But for now, Bitcoin is still very useful, and we shall talk about it.

3.   MONEY
SAVES MONEY

On its own, Bitcoin has no value, just as paper money is useless without any government backing. This government backing gives money the legitimacy or the promise that it can be used as a means of exchange for goods and services.

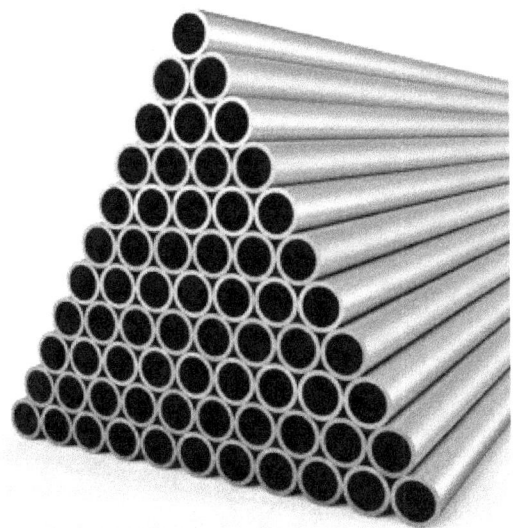

So why carry a pound of steel from USA to Canada when I can just take the equivalent in cash (which can easily fit into my pocket) which can be exchanged back to steel (money used to re-purchase steel) when I get to Canada. Money saves money. It will cost money to transport my steel from USA to Canada. This cost may be far higher than the price difference of steel between USA and Canada. So we have saved money by using money to purchase steel in Canada, instead of transporting steel to Canada.

In the same vein, Bitcoin became useful when it became possible to be able to exchange it to fiat currency, which in turn can be used to make purchases and payments. So, instead of do a bank wire transfer from USA to South Korea with huge bank charges, I can easily buy Bitcoin with my money in the US, send it to someone in South Korea, and this person can easily exchange it back to fiat currency in South Korea, with minimal fee.

This fee used to be in range of 1 cent to 1 USD. Whatever happened will be discussed later.

4. THE PROBLEM WITH BITCOIN

Bitcoin sending fee has become too high that people are already getting pissed off, and searching for alternatives. If people are already searching for alternatives, then it means you are late to the party already. But no, you are not, because the attraction to Bitcoin isn't just because of the low transaction charges.

We are not here to talk about the problems with Bitcoin. There are solutions, and we shall present those. Bitcoin transaction now takes forever to deliver, especially when you pay less fee. This is due to network confirmation taking too long to arrive. Now we are getting too deep for a beginner. Let's get back to the basics. People loved the idea of Bitcoin first because it was decentralized, could be used to make payments anonymously (for privacy reasons) and thirdly because it was very cheap to send money through the Bitcoin network.

The reason the fees has kept on rising over the years can be attributed to the fact that during every Bitcoin halving event, miners who dedicate their supercomputers and bandwith and electricity to power this amazing network would see their reward for mining a block slashed. The value of the BTC volume that served as fee in the past (0.001BTC may be worth $0.1 at that point) would be worth-less and miners accepted it, but the same value of BTC is now worth a fortune (0.001BTC now worth $60), and senders would complain to pay this as fee.

Anyone is free to pay a lower fee, but when miners are not able to break even (because it costs them money to mine Bitcoin), they will stop mining, and that creates more problems for the network. The few miners left will pick transactions with higher fees over transactions with lower fee (I wouldn't like to get into Satoshi per byte calculations, but it would be worth reading later). If your transaction with very low fee isn't picked up after a long time, the transaction could be declined. This is why everyone should be willing to pay a higher fee, and this continuous demand drives up the fee.

5.
INTRODUCTION

This course tries to simplify things without getting into more complex terms, and in areas where we have deviated, we would always point out that it is not important to know those. But it would always be a good idea to read, research and learn more as you gain more knowledge of the basic concepts.

Although we shall use token and coin interchangeably, there are few differences. A coin, just like Bitcoin must have its own blockchain, a term we shall treat later. A token (divided into utility and security tokens) can still be used in the same way that coins are used, but are built upon existing blockchains of another coin. Getting started with Bitcoin and other cryptocurrencies will be made easier if we know this.

1. Getting started with a wallet and the blockchain controversy
2. Learning about wallet addresses and network protocols
3. Finding out how to buy
4. Receiving the coin in your wallet
5. Trading in exchanges
6. Leverage Trades and Perpetual Futures
7. Altcoins
8. Sending from your wallet
9. Warnings on Tokenized Coins
10. Exploring the Blockchain
11. Securing your wallet
12. Non-fungible Token - NFT

We will try as much as possible to explain everything in detail, but as little as possible so as not to confuse a dummy. Please understand that you do not need to rely on advice gotten in this book. Talk to your financial adviser before you take any step. This is an honest disclaimer.

6. GETTING STARTED WITH A WALLET AND THE BLOCKCHAIN CONTROVERSY

The first thing you need to know about Bitcoin is how to store your Bitcoin. In 2021, there are countless apps and institutions you can use their facilities to host your wallet. You do not need a cold storage wallet anymore. One of the most popular wallet that you can use to store your Bitcoin is Blockchain.com wallet. Please note that this blockchain is different from the Blockchain technology that powers Bitcoin, much like how Apple (the company that makes iPhone) is different from the apple that you eat.

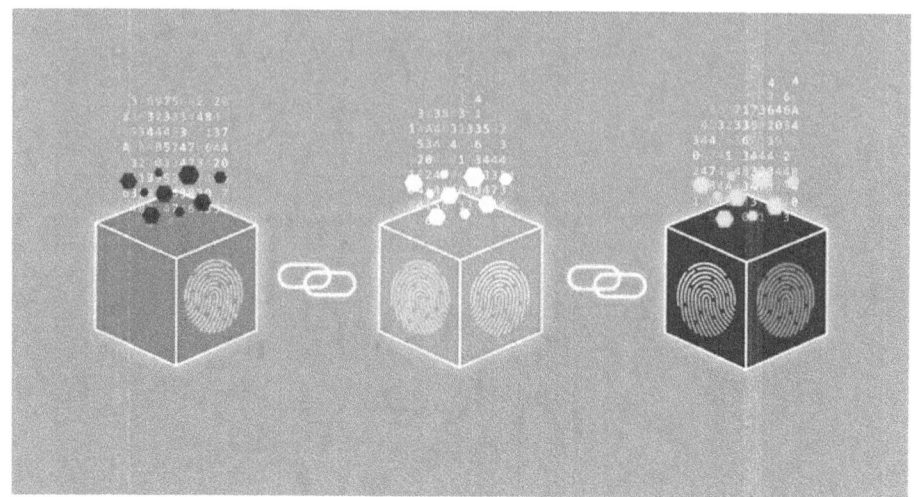

Blockchain as a technology refers to how digital transaction information can be collected in groups, and linked to each other, in such a way that these set of information (each block) is joined to form a chain. Each block has limit to the size of information it can store, which is why only a certain amount of transaction can be processed in every block, and miners always prioritize on the transactions with higher incentive (fee) leaving off the transactions with low fee to stay in a Limbo (known as mempool) for almost forever.

So, visit blockchain.com and sign up for a wallet. There are other wallet apps which you can download from app stores. You can also visit their websites. These popular wallets are:

- Trust Wallet
- Metamask
- Bitcoin.com
- Coinbase
- Trezor
- Electrum
- Exodus
- Luno
- Binance
- Bitfinex

- Blockchain
- Hotbit
- CoinGecko

Feel free to download anyone. A lot of these institutions offering wallet services are also exchanges. So you can use most of those apps to equally trade later.

A cold wallet is a cryptocurrency wallet that is not connected to the internet. It can also be called "Hardware wallet"or "Offline wallet". These are always considered to be more secure, because they are offline. This is surely not for a dummy.

You can also download Trading View for analytics.

7.

LEARNING ABOUT WALLET ADDRESSES AND NETWORK PROTOCOLS

Back in the days when it was just Bitcoin and a few other crypto-currencies, each cryptocurrency had its own network and that was just it. But now, things are becoming complicated. Let us just go ahead with Bitcoin, and later we treat other cryptocurrencies.

To create a Bitcoin wallet, find the instruction from the app or website or service you have decided to go with. A Bitcoin wallet address looks like this:

3QQVXHAtkrxK5aCZMQ2qPxRfE4hF-g7y9k2

You can see how unreadable a Bitcoin Wallet address is. So do not try to type it. Always copy and paste. Sometimes, they are converted to QR Code so that you can scan them.

A Bitcoin wallet address used to start with either 1 or 3, and used to be between 26 and 35 characters. But now, there are different protocols of Bitcoin wallet addresses.

There are P2PKH, P2SH and bech32. P2PKH starts with 1, P2SH starts with 3 while bech32 starts with bc1. You do not need to concern yourself with this issue, but you need to be able to recognize a Bitcoin wallet address when you see one. It is worth mentioning because I have seen people make mistake of copying email addresses or login IDs (of which Blockchain.com's base32 login ID looks like one) instead of a wallet address.

When you make a mistake in the address, some wallets will not send the fund, but it is better to learn how to recognize a Bitcoin Wallet address, than make the mistake that will cost a fortune. Apart from the protocols mentioned here, some wallets can show you different protocols while trying to create a wallet address. Binance will show you the options of going through the main BTC network (which has the highest fee) and a BEP20 (SC) which stands for Binance Smartchain, and ERC20. This smartchain should only be used when the receiving party has a similar address that supports such tokens. Trust Wallet for example supports most of those wrapped tokens.

Ethereum uses ERC20 wallet address, which looks like hexadecimal but starts with "0x" in it. USDT token can be issued through

ERC20, TRC20 and BEP20(SC) networks. There is also OMNI. These introduce some more complexity while generating wallet addresses. As a rule of thumb, always use the protocol native to a particular currency you are about to receive, unless the sender explicitly requests for a particular protocol.

- For Bitcoin (BTC), use the Bitcoin Network address.
- For Ethereum (ETH), use the ERC20 Network address.
- For TRON (TRX), use the TRC20 Network address.

You should also learn to do a test-transaction on addresses before moving a big sum.

NOTES ON TAGS AND MEMO: Depending on the coin or token, some will require more than just wallet address to send and receive. XLM for example can have an additional or optional Memo while XRP uses a tag. Find out from your wallet if you require to use a tag or memo to be able to receive any token.

8.   FINDING OUT HOW TO BUY

Buying a currency like Bitcoin opens us up to a whole lot of fraud, because sometimes, we can make the mistake of sending money to the wrong person without getting its equivalent in the cryptocurrency. To mitigate this, use P2P platforms that have done some sort of verifications for their users. You can also use your credit card to make purchases on Coinbase. How about how much you need to pay to get a certain coin? It's easy, no matter what your local currency is.

Most currencies are shown in their United States Dollar (USD) price. So assuming you need to buy 1BTC, and 1BTC to USD currently sits at 60,000 USD, all you need to do is check how much your local currency converts to in USD and use that to calculate how much of your local currency you need to set aside to buy 1BTC. Also remember to make 5% adjustment as you might be paying some fees depending on what medium you would be using to make the payment.

So if 1BTC=$60,000 but your local currency is Yuan.

$1 = 6.52 Yuan.

To buy 1BTC, you need 60,000 x 6.52 = 391,200 Yuan.

Adding an additional 5% in case there are fees, you need to get ready 5% of 391,200 Yuan which is 19,560 Yuan.

Total funds to get ready=391,200+19,560=410,760 Yuan.

But you do not need to buy 1BTC in case that sounds too expensive for you. Bitcoin can be split, as well as other cryptocurrencies. You can buy half which is 0.5 BTC. You can buy a quarter which is 0.25. In fact, you can buy any value as long as it doesn't go below what you need to pay in fee. For example, you cannot buy 0.00001 BTC when you require 0.0005 BTC as fee. It just doesn't make sense. But the point is that you can buy $100 worth of Bitcoin, or $20 or whatever you can afford.

To buy using P2P platforms, visit websites like Localbitcoin.com, Paxful and Binance, or use local Bitcoin ATM which can be found in many major cities where it is not illegal to use one. Usually, the platform you are using either delivers the Bitcoin in the wallet they operate for you (custodial wallet) or gives you the option of submitting your own wallet address.

9.

RECEIVING THE COIN IN YOUR WALLET AND WAITING FOR CONFIRMATION

Imagine being told that money has been sent to your bank account, but you login to your banking app to check and you do not find any money there. There is also a scenario where you see the money reflect in your ledger balance, but not in your available balance for spending. This also happens on the Bitcoin network.

When you submit your wallet to someone, and the person genuinely sends some coins to it, there are many reasons why you may not see the coin reflect in your wallet instantly. Some platforms can estimate the average number of transactions they have to process within a specific time, and the fees involved, and need to use that economically. So what these platforms do is wait at intervals (maybe 30 seconds, 1 minute, 5 minutes or as the case may be) to collect several transactions, and send them at once using the same single fee. And yes, in Bitcoin network, several addresses as well as a single address can be sent coin to, in one single transaction, from one address or from many addresses. So why would exchangers pay multiple fee when they can issue multiple transactions and pay just once? As they pack in more transaction (larger bytes), they need to increase the fee, but not to the extent of what would be paid if each transaction was handled individually.

So, probably you have not seen this coin reflect in your wallet because the sender has submitted it, but the financial institution hasn't processed it. Once this transaction is pushed to the Bitcoin network, it stays in a mempool. The mempool is where all valid transactions wait to be checked for authenticity by the Bitcoin network, before the recipient can be allowed to spend it.

So when your coin is in the mempool, it may show up in your wallet as incoming, but you cannot spend it because it is unconfirmed. Some wallets will allow you be able to spend your coin after 1 confirmation, and some after 2 confirmations while others will wait for 3 confirmations. These confirmations are important to avoid double-spending scam. With more confirmations increases the difficulty of double-spending. So if you have to pay someone you do not know after you have received your Bitcoin, make sure the Bitcoin is confirmed at least once before releasing payment to the person.

Network confirmation can take a long time, especially when the fee paid to send the coin is low. Always understand that the conversion value of your coin can change while waiting for confirmation. For example, if 1 BTC is sent to you today (when 1BTC converts to 60,000USD) but you receive it tomorrow (when Bitcoin now trades at 55,000USD) you have lost 5,000 USD while waiting for confirmation. This explanation is also to guide you, in case you need to pay for the coin based on its value when received. It is considered received only after confirmation.

If you do not want to get into such losses, opt to receive a stable token like USDT, TUSD, USDC or BUSD. These are tokens that will maintain the same value with real fiat currencies, although this promise is not guaranteed because some of the institutions that issue these tokens refuse to be audited. But while waiting for confirmation, the opposite could happen and your coin rises in value. A perfect example of "My Time is money".

10. TRADING IN EXCHANGES

Trading is what almost anyone who wants to make money online does, so we shall treat it. But remember, there is always a disclaimer not to use this as financial advice. Consult your financial adviser before taking any step, as trading is risky. You can lose some of your money, or even all of your money while trading.

That said, if you still insist, let us go ahead. Most trading platforms (not all) will let you have many accounts (also known as sub-accounts) within a single wallet app. The aim of these many accounts is to make it easy for you to separate different funds for different purposes. Since you are taking a risk while trading, you should be able to determine what amount you wish to risk, and have a way of ensuring you do not have to make the mistake of using more than you wish to risk. You can also look at these accounts like partitions or rooms within your house. You are leaving your house full of kids and you have 10 bars of chocolate. You want the kids to eat 3 bars, and you know they will eat just 3 bars. But to leave little room for error, you lock up the remaining 7 bars in a separate room where the kids cannot get into.

On Binance, one can have several sub-accounts. Within each account, there is a spot wallet, margin wallet, futures wallet, savings wallet, pool wallet, P2P wallet etc. You can conveniently transfer your funds from one wallet to another without incurring any fees, as long as they are within the same main wallet/ account.

To transfer, all you need to do is click on wallet, navigate to the wallet type you wish to operate on, touch transfer button, select the FROM and the TO as well as the currency to be transferred. Enter the amount or click the MAX button to enter everything you have for the selected coin in the FROM wallet. Click on the transfer button and the funds will be transferred.

So, if you want to trade on the spot market with 0.01 BTC but you have 1BTC in your spot wallet, you need to transfer out 0.99BTC to a different wallet, and nothing will happen to that fund. This is to make sure that while trying to sell 0.01 BTC, you don't make a mistake and sell 0.1BTC. And if the platform you use does not have anything like this, I wish you best of luck typing numbers, and making no mistake about that.

To view a wide range of all available markets and trading pairs, Click on Market/Exchange on your trading app. There should be a way to select the particular pair you wish to checkout. To sell your BTC and get USDT, Select the BTC/USDT spot market. Either set the rate you wish to sell your BTC (limit price) or use the current market rate to sell it.

In the case of BTC/USDT pair, **Rate**, also known as price, is the total amount of USDT you are willing to pay or get for a unit (1) of a currency (BTC).

Remember to always sell higher than you bought. If BTC was bought at a rate of $60,000, try and sell when it gets to $65,000 and wait for it to fall again before you buy. Do not sell lower than you bought, unless you feel it will fall further and you wish to buy when it is at its lowest so that you can sell when it rises.

Please refer to the steps in buying XRP below for more details on buying and selling which basically is what trading is.

To buy any coin on Binance, follow these steps:

- Click on Wallet
- Navigate to Spot
- Scroll to the coin you wish to buy and click on it. Example: XRP.
- You will see different currency pairs you can use to purchase XRP. Example: XRP/BTC, XRP/USDT. If you have BTC, you should click on the former. If you have USDT, click on the later.
- Buy icon (always in green colour) will already be highlighted. If not, click on Buy, select limit, enter buy price (rate), buy quantity (volume) and click on BUY.
- Note: Buy price should match market price to close the deal immediately. If you do not know how to read the market price, change that "limit" to "market" and the coin will be purchased instantly.

To sell any coin is pretty much the same process as buying. Selling colour is always in red. You do not have to use the market price for all your trades. You can read a graph, make some prediction of where a currency will be after some time, then set your buying or selling price to that limit and go to sleep. If it works out, you try it again, and keep taking profits. If it does not, know when to cut your losses.

11.

LEVERAGE TRADES AND PERPETUAL FUTURES

Spot trading is the most common type of trading where you use exactly what you have to trade without any loans, leverage or margin of any type, and you get your assets delivered immediately. It is highly unlikely to get your ass kicked so fast while doing this, but it is also very unlikely to grow very quickly. So what do (greedy) people do? They leverage on loans to trade so as to quickly grow their money, but are likely to lose it all.

I have nothing against being greedy. To get greedy, keep reading about this leverage.

On Binance, transfer your USDT Coin to your Futures wallet. Go to trades and select the futures market, BTC/USDT. You will see leverage, usually labelled with x1. Touch it. You will see x1 to x100. On Bitmex, leverage can equally get to x125. If you select x100, it means that the funds you are using to trade will be made to increase, up to 100 times the value of your capital. If you had about $1,000 worth of BTC, you could trade with $100,000 worth of BTC and this means that a 1% change in BTC value can either double your capital or make you lose your capital. Therefore, you do not need to select x100. You can start with x2 or x5 and then get to x25 when you can understand the market movement better. It is not a good idea to go beyond x25. There are professionals that claim to give signals of when a currency is more likely to rise or fall. Certain people get these signals and feel confident about them, hence the need for x100.

In the futures market, you may find it confusing as a beginner because instead of BUY or SELL, what you find here is SHORT and LONG.

Long Vs Short Positions in Forex

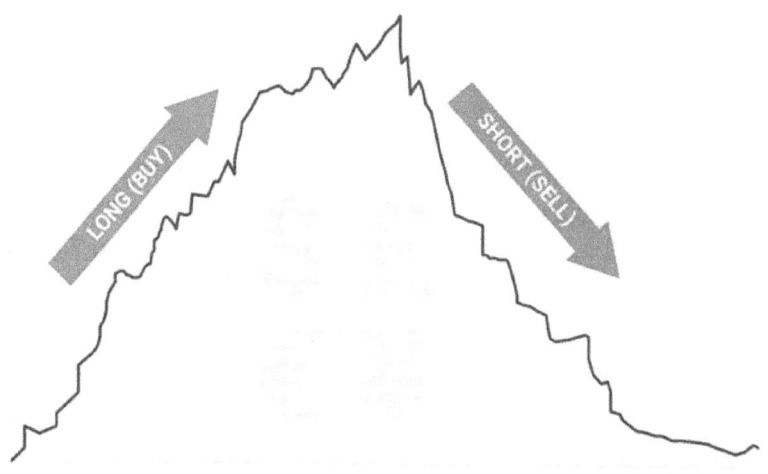

Short is like a bet that the currency will fall in value, and as it falls, you make money. Long is like a bet that the currency will rise in value, and as it rises, you make money. But if it moves against your bet, you lose money in the same proportion as you would gain if it had moved in your favour. So instead of simply buying or selling a currency, Shorting or Longing refers to the position you can take.

When you buy into this position (when you buy a currency with certain prediction of a rise or fall), you will be able to see your profit or loss in real-time at an area labelled with PNL (which stands for Profit and Loss). Once you find a profit you can take, you close the position and heave a sigh. If the losses start eating too deep into your capital, you should also know when to exit and cut your losses. Liquidation is the final action when your loss equals your collateral (original capital before the leverage).

There are tutorials on this when you visit the Binance academy website. Remember that trading is risky. Trade at your own risk.

Wondering how the money is made when a currency rises as well as when it falls?

In the case of Bitcoin. If you believe Bitcoin will rise, you hold your Bitcoin and only sell after it rises. This Long Position means you have to buy Bitcoin before it starts rising. This is why Long is also known as BUY. But if you feel the price of Bitcoin will fall, you need to sell the Bitcoin you have, and wait for it to fall so that you can re-buy. Assuming you sold 1 BTC and got $60,000 and you are expecting it to fall, when it falls to $55,000, you can buy the same 1 BTC and have $5,000 which is now your free money a.k.a profit. This is why people borrow to get into a long and short position. If you borrowed x10 of your capital, instead of gain $5,000, you will gain $50,000. And if you borrowed x100, you will gain $500,000.

Also note that different exchanges have different trading fees. So you pay to get into any position, or to make any trade. Binance charges a fee as high as 0.1% of the value of currency you are trading. So if a currency appreciates by 0.1% and you make a move, you are simply using your profit to pay trading fee. Get your numbers right before you make any move.

12.   ALTCOINS

Bitcoin is the first cryptocurrency that gained massive adoption and its market capitalization is more than all the other cryptocurrencies combined. Therefore, any cryptocurrency that isn't Bitcoin is just an alternative to Bitcoin, also known as Altcoin.

There are countless altcoins and tokens in existence today:

- Ethereum ETC
- Stellar XLM
- Tron TRX
- Ripples XRP
- Dogecoin DOGE
- Litecoin LTC
- Binance Coin BNB
- Bittorent Token BTT

Etc.

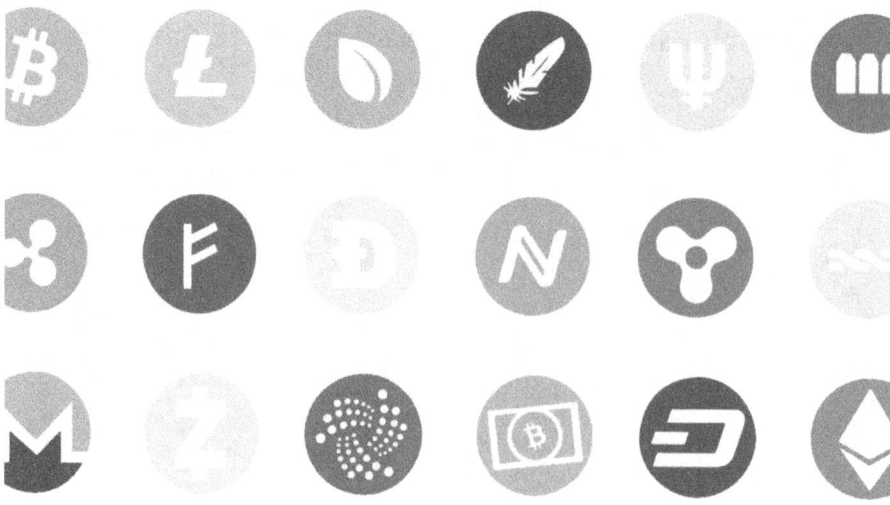

Some of these coins present a better alternative to Bitcoin, both in how cheap they are to send and receive, and how fast the transactions are. Some can also be used to implement smart contracts. You see why Bitcoin, if it does not continue to evolve, might just phase out. Bitcoin has had many upgrades, and that's what gave birth to Bitcoin Cash. Little changes to the network protocol (soft fork) may lead to no new currency being formed, but when a massive change (hard fork) comes, some people may prefer to stick to the old currency and its rules while others move along with the new changes, and this usually causes a branch which fork represents. Ethereum Classic used to be the main Ethereum before it branched and new changes were made to form the Ethereum that has now become a currency on its own. The branch with the wider adoption always retain the original name of the coin.

Today, many cryptocurrencies are created with their own protocols described in a white paper, and so many people buy into it in what is called an initial coin offering (ICO), much like a company going public in an initial public offering (IPO). Several coins don't make it past the ICO before dying off – these are known as dead coins. Those that have survived go on to either become worthless over time, or keep rising in value. Today, XLM is at $0.40. It is affordable to buy these little coins and tokens and save them for the future. If in the future the tokens and coins become useful, your story might turn out to sound like that of so many that bought Bitcoin when it exchanged for 8 cents in 2010.

There is also another strategy one could use to buy some of these altcoins with prospects, without breaking the bank. This strategy is known as Dollar Cost Averaging (DCA). This is a way of putting out a fixed amount at intervals to purchase coins for keeping (or holding or hodling). You need to spend so little that it shouldn't affect your income and expenses, and you shouldn't be bothered if the currency starts to drop in value. The target is the long term when the currency is likely to climb over time.

13.   SENDING
FROM YOUR WALLET

It is important to understand how you can send your Bitcoin from your wallet to the wallet address of someone else. You already learned what a Wallet address looks like.

3QQVXHAtkrxK5aCZMQ2qPxRfE4hF-g7y9k2

Because you can either copy and paste a wallet, or scan a code, there are scenarios where you have the QR code in your own device, but not the address, and your device camera cannot scan what is inside of it. What you should do is use another device to scan it, then use messaging apps to send the details to your own device. What if you don't have two phones ready? Some scanners exist on the playstore which can scan a picture in your gallery. These kinds of apps become handy in this situation.

Go ahead and copy the wallet address above, or scan the QR code, and you will see that they both show the same thing.

Click on Send or Withdrawal button in your app, paste or scan the wallet address. Enter the amount you are requesting to withdraw or send. Remember that some wallets may deduct the network fee from your total sending amount while other wallets will deduct it from your balance. However, if you have no balance, the sending amount is likely to be adjusted. Some wallets will also show you network protocols. If the address you are sending Bitcoin to is not like the usual address I described, do not proceed, you may have been given a TRC20 wallet, BEP20 (SC) wallet or an ERC20 wallet. Ask the person who sent the wallet to you before proceeding.

But if you have the option to request for any type of address, use BEP20 (SC) to save on fee and save on time. You don't want the recipient to be waiting for the coin to arrive forever and ever. Check the next chapter before using those cheap networks though.

Once you are done sorting out the fees and addresses and protocols, most wallets will ask for authentication to complete the sending. Provide the required authentication and then watch the funds leave your wallet.

Please remember to ask the recipient if a memo or tag is required for any address you are sending funds to, to avoid any potential losses. XLM and XRP require an optional memo and tag respectively.

14.   WARNINGS ON TOKENIZED COINS

I had advised on strategies one could use to save on fees. But there are also dangers to this fee-saving strategy. Before we look into these risks, let us look at tokens like USDT. The idea behind stable coin like USDT means locking real world asset worth a certain amount of USD, and minting exactly the same quantity in a network like TRON TRC20 or ETHEREUM ERC20 or BINANCE SMARTCHAIN BEP20. So, if there is a mechanism to lock $1m worth of real world asset by a company such as Tether Foundation, same 1m USDT can be minted as USDT on ERC20, or TRC20 or divided amongst the two networks depending on where there is more demand for the token. Given that TRC20 uses lesser fee than ERC20, there might be more demand for the USDT on TRC20. So the issuing body (Tether Foundation) may decide to mint 600,000 USDT on the TRC20 network and 400,000 USDT on the ERC20 network. Note that this issuing body is trusted with ensuring that every USDT can be redeemed when needed for the promised Dollar value. This is why they must ensure that every minted USDT is backed by at least $1 in cash or in asset. You have to trust Tether Foundation to be able to keep to their words.

This method of tokenizing real world assets is also employed in tokenizing coins like Bitcoin and even Ethereum. Binance as a company can lock a certain amount of Bitcoin, say 1000BTC, and issue the same value in a BEP20 network token, maybe with the name Binance-Pegged Bitcoin (BTCB). The advantage of doing this is that one can now send the newly issued Bitcoin to any BEP20 address using BNB as gas fees – a fee that is already way cheaper than what is spent sending real-world Bitcoin. This is synonymous to the gain achieved in our steel example in a previous chapter. But just as we need to trust the government to ensure the notes we carry maintain a certain value, we need to trust the body issuing these tokens to not joke around with the locked assets. The Dollar used to be backed by real gold. But the failure to maintain this parity may have contributed to the inflation affecting the Dollar today.

Therefore, the Bitcoin that goes through the BEP20 network is just a tokenized Bitcoin that may or may not be redeemed for the original Bitcoin when the time comes. Anytime the original asset is redeemed (unlocked), the tokens are to be destroyed, just the opposite of what was done when they were minted (and the real world asset was locked). The process should therefore be reversible. It is up to the issuing body to keep to their words of pegging the value of the minted token with the real world asset.

But this same issue of distrust confronts those who trade on most Centralized Exchanges like Binance, Bitfinex and Bitmex. If the owners of these platforms decide to elope tomorrow with customers' funds, possibly, these funds may never be recovered. This is why it is often said that if you don't control the private keys to the wallet that holds your coin, it is not your coin. Most coins are held in custodial wallets, and the keys are controlled by the exchanges. This same risk is faced while using tokenized coins like BTCB, BETH, wBTC etc.

Decentralized exchanges (Dex) are springing up every day. These Dexes allow trading directly from your wallet, and each transaction is publicly recorded on the Blockchain. The fact that this recorded transaction will have to be validated therefore attracts transaction fees. The transaction fees go to both the liquidity providers and the network.

Example of these Dexes are:
- Uniswap – app.uniswap.org
- Pancakeswap – pancakeswap.finance

- SushiSwap – sushi.com
- Apeswap – apeswap.finance

15.

EXPLORING THE BLOCKCHAIN

Blockchain is already explained as link of blocks, with each blocks containing information, and these information are simply transactions. How can we dig into this transaction, especially due to the fact that some wallets do not give us access to this, and partly because we are some curious cats? Blockchain.com Company will be helpful in this regards. There are other Bitcoin blockchain explorers, but I like blockchain.com for its simplicity. I can use this explorer to monitor transactions in and out of any wallet. Four things to note in every transactions are: Sending address (input address), receiving address (output address), network fee (gas fee) and transaction ID (Transaction hash).

We can lookup a transaction by its transaction ID or by a wallet address. This is why the search bar on Blockchain.com explorer will ask for either wallet address or transaction ID.

https://www.blockchain.com/explorer

Explorer › ⬡ Bitcoin Explorer ▾ › Address   🔍 search your transaction, an address or a block   USD ▾

To lookup a wallet address, simply paste the wallet address in that search bar or enter it in the following the address

https://www.blockchain.com/btc/address/
PasteWalletAddressHere

Example: https://www.blockchain.com/btc/
address/1CZnZuX99k9gLGeVQDWHCc1nePyRuQJbnZ

From the information below, you can see total transaction carried out by this address. You can see total amount received, total sent out and final balance. When you click on the USD/BTC tab, you can toggle the unit of the currency being shown.

When you scroll further down, you will see transactions where green colour represents credit while red represents debit.

A transaction can come from several input addresses, and go to several output addresses. It can also come from a single input address and go to a single output address. Finally, a transaction can come from a single input address and be distributed to multiple output addresses. We have talked about how fees can be changed using this style, although most times, these are done by the wallet management companies.

You can also see when a transaction hits the blockchain but is still unconfirmed in the mempool. Check the screenshot below:

You can see that this transaction is still unconfirmed. To see all the details of any particular transaction, and not the overview of every transaction shown for a wallet, click the Hash. You can also copy the Transaction hash or ID from your wallet and paste in the search bar of blockchain.com

The web address format for exploring each transaction is: https://www.blockchain.com/btc/tx/PasteTheHashHere.

Example: https://www.blockchain.com/btc/tx/d834c4372e5883874cdcf92ae0bba216833949f3d3affae-2ceac3da6558aec59

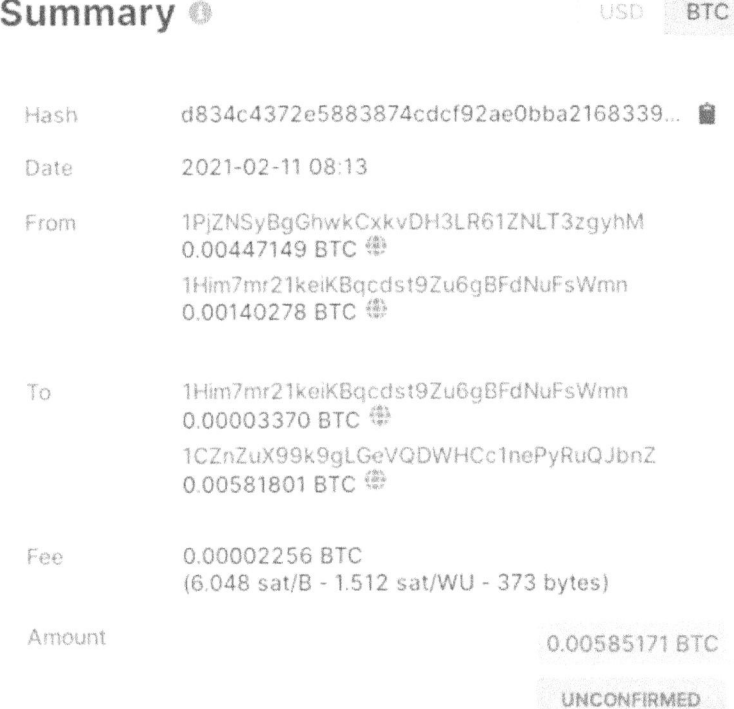

As you scroll further down, you will see more details, including USD value when the transaction was initiated.

Status	Unconfirmed
Received Time	2021-02-11 08:13
Size	373 bytes
Weight	1,492
Included in Block	Mempool
Confirmations	0
Total Input	0.00587427 BTC
Total Output	0.00585171 BTC
Fees	0.00002256 BTC
Fee per byte	6.048 sat/B
Fee per weight unit	1.512 sat/WU
Value when transacted	$263.98

Please note that even as exchanges send your Bitcoin through the network, sometimes they do not exactly process your send/withdrawal transaction directly from your wallet. As a result, sometimes you see fund leave your wallet address in explorer, but your balance in your wallet app stays the same. This is why some of them will let you know that the wallet address they give you is also known as Receiving address only. This means that while sending, they can decide to fulfill your send transaction from a couple of other addresses.

Now that you have learnt everything about blockchain exploring, you can monitor any address or lookup any transaction you wish to on the Bitcoin network.

You can also look up transactions on:

- Bitcoin network on blockchair.com
- TRC20 network on tronscan.org
- ERC20 network on etherscan.io
- BEP20 network on bscscan.com

There are publicly available explorers for almost every blockchain that exists.

16.   SECURING YOUR WALLET

Remember that Bitcoin is money, at least until it stops being worth anything. You need to be security conscious when handling them. You need to take lots of steps to secure your wallet. There is no risk in anyone having your wallet addresses (you can have multiple addresses). An address is like a bank account number, and does not need to be guarded. But the wallet from where you send out funds, and receive funds, need to be guarded. Many wallet apps do this by asking you to note down some words known as mnemonics or passphrase, which can be used to encrypt and decrypt your private key. You save these sets of words. Should you lose access to your wallet, you will need them to regain access to use your funds. Write the passphrase on a piece of paper and save in at least three secure locations. Should anything happen to one location, or two at the same time due to some weird coincidence, you use the one in third location to duplicate and distribute again.

It is also important to use some forms of authentication before you send out Bitcoin, so that if anyone accidentally gets hold of your device, the person would not be able to send funds out of your wallet.

Google authenticator is also used for One Time Password generation which you can use to authorize any transaction. If your wallet offers any of these two factor authentications, including SMS and email OTP, please activate them. But all these would be useless if they are all on the same compromised device. This is one of the reasons why you must lock the wallet app so that no one can open it to even view your balance.

Note: There are many coins that can no longer be accessed today, partly because some owners lost their access details, while other owners are just no longer alive. Wouldn't you want someone to get access to your coin should anything happen to you? Find a way to present all the access details so that your next of kin would be able to find it and put your coin to good use. We are not going to stay here forever.

I wish you best of luck in your trading endeavor.

17.   NON-FUNGIBLE TOKEN - NFT

Fungibility is a quality of an item that ensures it can be replaced by another identical item. Fungibility implies equal value between items. For example, you can lend me a dollar bill today. Tomorrow I return a different dollar bill to you, and you will have to accept it because the dollar is fungible. Any one dollar bill can be used in place of any other dollar bill for any transaction. Bitcoin is fungible. There is no difference between the first mined Bitcoin and another. A token like USDT is also fungible. The first group of USDT minted on the TRON network is no different from the last token. USDT is therefore a fungible token.

Now Non-Fungible Token. You already know what a token is. You already know what fungible means. There has been a lot of hype around Non-fungible tokens. Just like any other token, a new token can be created on any supported blockchain like the Ethereum network. This new token simply represents a real-world object that is digitally hosted somewhere. This digital item could be a Tweet, a photo, a video clip, an image/picture, a music clip, a document, or just anything that can be uploaded on the internet. The token will contain information such as the URI/link to the item it represents, which wallet address first owned it, if it has been transferred to any other wallet address, the current wallet address holding it, and how much was used to purchase it. This is NFT in a nutshell. It is cryptographic, unique, one of a kind, digital art, issued by the authentic owner.

That you own an NFT does not mean that no one else can own it too. The owner might decide to mint as many as is required. But each piece is unique and cannot be replaced with the other. A picture or video that you own as an NFT can also be duplicated freely all over the internet. The NFT version in your wallet is just a proof of ownership or much like a certificate. It means that you own the authentic version. In fact, there are possibilities that you may just hold a certificate of a lost item if the photo/video gets deleted from the server where it is hosted. This is why you also have to worry about the future availability of where your digital file is currently hosted. The certificate of ownership is in the blockchain, but not the actual art.

NFT will become a new way to showcase wealth, just like the rich and famous attend global art exhibitions and pay so much money for a chance to own famous artworks. If you still have doubts over NFTs, look at this excerpt from Arthur Hayes.

Rock, Paper, Scissors Says GO!
By. Arthur Hayes - 20 Aug 2021

As social beings, the sole purpose of many activities and purchases is to publicly display how much energy you can waste. The nightclub economy is extremely a propos to this concept. Individuals walk into a dark room, listen to loud music (art), dance (a waste of energy akin to a mating call), and pay exorbitant amounts of money to drink liquid. Everyone gets dressed up real nice in articles of clothing that serve no useful purpose other than to demonstrate that the wearer spent a lot of money to display their social status to the rest of the clubbers present.

If you think nightclubs are too gauche, then how about a global art exhibit? The rich and famous art lovers, creators, and curators waste energy travelling to one place. They congregate to "collect" useless paintings, sculptures, and other installations. There is a definite social pecking order based on the gallery you represent and/or how many pieces of useless stuff you hoard. Food and drink are provided to socialise with other like-minded enlightened art aficionados, and when finished, everyone packs up and wastes more energy returning to their homes.

Socialisation and communication are why humans are special. That's how we build monuments to our gods and rulers. That's how we put a man on the moon. That's how we created the internet and integrated circuits. Flexing is both a 100% waste of energy, and essential to creating the social bonds that allow civilisation to progress.

Flexing is integral to the human experience. We don't question the value of physical meatspace items used to project social standing. We understand and value fashion, paintings, jewelry etc. We all don costumes at work that illustrate which professional community we belong to. What is an investment banker without his Hermes tie or her pair of red-soled Louboutins? The costume is part of the self-worth.

Just because robots take all of our meatspace jobs doesn't mean that humans stop being humans in the metaverse. Social signaling will take new forms powered by blockchain enabled NFT "worthless" objects. Those who recognise the similarities and are early to the creation of a new market for digital Flex goods will reap astronomical returns. Those content to pooh pooh this new worthless form of social signal can continue to walk down a street, into a shop, and purchase a $500 white t-shirt from some well-marketed fashion house. Choose your Flex Good appropriately.

Scalable Flexing is a tech person's dream. The ability to appear wealthy and cool is not limited to physical proximity, but the entire addressable market of your avatar.

To get started with NFTs, visit the following apps/websites:
- binance.com/en/nft/home

- rarible.com
- opeansea.io
- etherrock.com
- cryptokitties.co
- larvalabs.com/cryptopunks

Just like fungible tokens, do not buy NFT with a cryptocurrency you cannot afford to lose. Invest wisely. Think about selling NFTs rather than buying.

GOOD LUCK